PO TBUVSEBZ

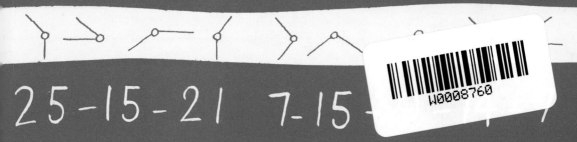

25-15-21 7-15-

.- / – / ... / .. – ... – / – / .... . / . – . / – / – . – – /

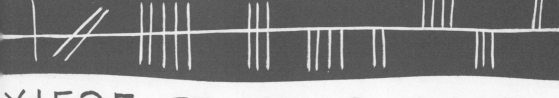

XIFSF JT UIF QJDOJD

ISWAY ITWAY

11- 35- 35- 42- 34- 11- 13- 23- 24 - 33 - 22

FRANKLIN WATTS, INC.

575 LEXINGTON AVENUE
NEW YORK 22, N. Y.

The FIRST BOOK of

CODES and CIPHERS

GSV URIHG YLLP LU
XLWVH ZMW XRKSVIH

YB HZN ZMW YVIBO VKHGVRM
KRXG FIVH YB OZHAOL ILGS

BY SAM and BERYL EPSTEIN

Pictures by LÁSZLO ROTH

DMVC NFFUJOH UPEBZ

SBN 531-00502-X

Copyright © 1956 by Franklin Watts, Inc.

Printed in the United States of America.

by The Garrison Corp.

Library of Congress Catalog Card Number: 56-9134

14   15

18-9-7-8-20
1-6-20-5-18
19-3-8-15-15-12

12.

EREWHAY ILLWAY OUYAY EBAY AFTERWAY OOLSCHAY ?

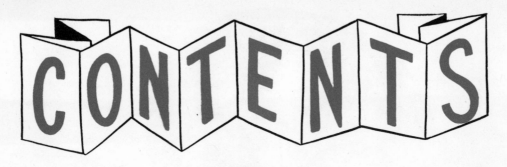

CONTENTS

Keeping secrets

If you have a secret that you want only one or two special friends to know, and no one else, you will probably be very cautious about writing it down. But if you write your secret in code, or in a special language, or in invisible ink, you can be sure it will be safe.

In the following pages, you will learn some codes that you and your friends can use for sending each other secret messages that no one else will be able to understand. You will also learn a secret language with which to speak to each other. And you will find out how to use ordinary things around the house to make ink which becomes invisible after you have written with it.

Codes of many kinds have played an important part in the history of the world. Kings, soldiers, spies, pirates, and all kinds of people have used codes and secret writing for hundreds of years. This book will tell you about some of them.

Your first code

Here is a quick and easy way for you and a friend to send secret messages to each other.

First each person must take a clean sheet of paper and print the alphabet across the top, like this:

A B C D E F G H I J K L M N O P Q R S T U V W X Y Z

Leave some space below the alphabet, and then write the message that you want to send to your friend. Let's say that you want to tell him MEET ME AFTER SCHOOL.

Now you are ready to put that message into the secret code. This is called **encoding** the message.

Leave some space below the real message, so that you will be writing your encoded message near the bottom of the sheet.

The first letter in your real message is the letter M. Find that letter in the alphabet. Then look at the letter after it. You will see that the letter after M is N. Write down N as the first letter in your encoded message.

The next letter in your real message is E. As the letter after E is F, put an F as the second letter in your encoded message. The third letter will be F too, because there are two E's in the original message. Now there is only one letter left in the first word of the original message—the letter T. Look at the alphabet once more and you will see that the letter after T is U. So write the letter U as the fourth letter in your encoded message.

Now you have written one whole word of the encoded message. It looks like this: NFFU.

Write the other words of the message in the same way. The second word, ME, will be written as NF, because N is the letter after M and F is the letter after E.

AFTER will be written as BGUFS, because B is the letter after A, G is the letter after F, U is the letter after T, F is the letter after E, and S is the letter after R.

To put the word SCHOOL into code do the same thing: always write down the letter *after* the one in the original word. The word

SCHOOL will look like this: TDIPPM.

When your encoded message is finished it will look like this: NFFU NF BGUFS TDIPPM.

Now carefully tear off the bottom of the sheet of paper—the part where you have written the encoded message — and you are ready to send it.

Of course your friend can read the secret message only if he knows your code. Reading an encoded message is called **decoding** it. This is how your friend will decode the message:

He will look at the first letter in the encoded message and see that it is N, and he knows that the first letter in the real message must be the letter that comes before N in the alphabet. By looking at his own alphabet he will see that the letter before N is M. So he will write an M underneath the N in your message.

Then he will look at the alphabet and find out what letter comes before F. He will see that the letter is E, and so he will write an E underneath the F. He will write another E under the second F. And he will look at the alphabet and find that the letter before U is T. When he writes the letter T under the U he has decoded the first word of the message. He knows that the first word is MEET.

He will figure out the other words of the message in the same way, always writing down the letter that comes in the alphabet *before* the letter in your encoded message.

When he has finished decoding the message it will look like this:

NFFU   NF   BGUFS   TDIPPM.
MEET   ME   AFTER   SCHOOL.

Just remember that when you want to put a message into this

code, you always write the letter that comes *after* the letter in the original message. And when you receive a message in this code, and want to decode it, you always write down the letter that comes *before* the letter in the secret message.

Here is a good way to practice using this code. Take a fresh sheet of paper, print the alphabet at the top, and put these messages into code:

Club meeting today
Call for me on saturday

Now decode this message:

XIFSF JT UIF QJDOJD

Look on answer page 57, and you will see whether you encoded and decoded the messages correctly.

One thing to remember: when the letter z appears in a real message, you can't put that letter into code in the usual way, because there is no letter after z in the alphabet. So go back to the beginning of the alphabet and use the letter A as the code letter for z. And when you find the letter A in a secret message, remember that it is the code letter for z.

This alphabet code is very easy to use, because whenever you want to encode or decode a message, all you have to do is print the alphabet at the top of a sheet of paper and go to work.

Codes and ciphers

There are three basic kinds of secret writing. One is the invisible writing that you can read about on page 44. The other two kinds are called codes and ciphers.

The words **code** and **cipher** have separate meanings. Look in the dictionary and you will see that a **code** is a method of writing in which each individual word is written as a secret code word, code number, or symbol. Here, for example, is part of a real code:

for the word TROOPS use WHITE
for the word GUNS use GREEN
for the word CANNON use YELLOW
for the word BRIDGE use PURPLE
for the word ORDER use BLACK
for the word TO use PINK

An army commander who has a code like that could send out a message which says: BLACK WHITE YELLOW PINK PURPLE. And only another army officer who knows the code would be able to understand the message. As you can easily see, the message really says: ORDER TROOPS and CANNON TO BRIDGE. (Unimportant words like "and" are sometimes omitted in a code message if the message will be perfectly clear without them.)

When George Washington set up a spy system during the American Revolution, his spies used a code for sending him information about the movements and strength of the enemy. The spies used certain numbers for certain words, and each spy had to have a code book which told him the code number for every word he might want to use.

These code books were made very simply. To make such a book, the man who invented the code sat down with a dictionary, and copied off into a notebook all the words a spy might have to use in his messages. Then he numbered the words in order. The number written alongside each word was the code for that word. Here are a few lines from a code book actually used by Washington's spies:

War	*680*
Was	*681*
We	*682*
Will	*683*
With	*684*

A real code is very difficult to "break," as experts say. (To break a code means to figure out the meaning of every code word, number, or symbol.) There are probably many codes used in the world today that have never been broken.

But there is one difficulty with using real codes. In order to use a real code, it is necessary to have a code book, because nobody could ever remember symbols or numbers or code words for every word he might want to send in a message. And of course if a code book is lost, or stolen, the person who finds it or steals it can read any message sent in that code.

The captain of a Navy ship in wartime, for example, must have a code book for encoding and decoding messages about his action against the enemy, and guarding that book is one of his most important responsibilities. He keeps the book bound in sheets of lead, which make it very heavy, and if the captain thinks his ship is about to be captured it is his duty to throw the code book overboard. The lead cover will make it sink to the bottom of the sea where no enemy can ever find it.

It is because code books are sometimes lost, or stolen, that many military men, and other people who wish to send secret messages, prefer to use the method of secret writing which experts call a **cipher.** A cipher is a system of secret writing in which every letter, instead of every word, has its secret symbol.

The alphabet code you just read about, beginning on page 3, is not really a code at all, but a cipher. It doesn't use a code word for each word in the real message. Instead it uses a code letter for each letter of the words in the real message. That "alphabet code,"

9

as we have called it, should really be called an "alphabet cipher."

Most people use the word "code" to mean either a code or a cipher, but if you want to learn a great deal about both codes and ciphers, remember that technically there is a difference between the two. A **cipher** substitutes a secret *letter* or some other kind of sign for every *letter* in the original message; a **code** substitutes a secret *word* or some other kind of sign for every *word* in the original message.

More alphabet ciphers

There are many different kinds of alphabet ciphers. Here is another one:

Instead of moving ahead one letter in the alphabet, when you **encipher** a message (that is, put it into cipher), move ahead two letters. To encipher the word CANDY, for example, first print the alphabet at the top of a sheet of paper. At the end of the alphabet also print the first two letters of a second alphabet, like this:

A B C D E F G H I J K L M N O P Q R S T U V W X Y Z A B

Now write your message underneath the alphabet—the word CANDY. Then, below the C, write the letter that comes second after C in the alphabet. This is the letter E. Below the A write the second letter after A, which is C. Below the N write the second letter after N, which is P. Below the D write the second letter after D, which is F. And below the Y write the second letter after Y, which is A. Your enciphered message will be: E C P F A.

If you receive a message written in this cipher you will also have to print an alphabet with two extra letters at the end, so that if the letters A or B appear in the message, you will be able to count back from those letters.

To decipher the message E Q O G, for example, write those four letters below your printed, extra-long alphabet. Then count *back* two letters from the E and you will come to the letter C. Write a C below the E. Then count back two letters from Q and you will come to the letter O. Write an O below the Q. Counting back two letters from O gives you M, and counting back two letters from G gives you E. Your deciphered message is: COME.

To practice this cipher, write the alphabet plus an extra A and B at the top of a sheet of paper and encipher this message:

IS YOUR HOMEWORK DONE ?

Now decipher this message:

K HKPKUJGF VJG DQQM

You will find the first message correctly enciphered, and the second message correctly deciphered, on answer page 57.

11

If you use the same cipher all the time, somebody may figure it out, so it is a good idea to be able to use more than one. If somebody has guessed that you are enciphering your messages by moving ahead one letter, or two letters, you might try moving ahead three letters, or four letters, or five letters.

When you encipher messages by moving ahead three letters, you have to add the three letters A B C to the end of your alphabet. When you move ahead four letters, you have to add the four letters A B C D to the end of your alphabet. If you are going to move ahead five letters, you must add the five letters A B C D E to the end of your alphabet. In each case the person who deciphers your messages must add the same number of letters to his alphabet that you add to yours.

But if you change your cipher—if, instead of moving ahead two letters, you decide to move ahead four letters, for example, be sure to tell the friend who receives your message what cipher you used. Otherwise he will not be able to decipher the message.

Caesar's cipher

Julius Caesar, the famous Roman general who conquered almost all of Europe about 2,000 years ago, used an alphabet cipher when he sent secret messages to his generals. The cipher he used is one you have just learned: he moved ahead in the alphabet, and wrote D instead of A, E instead of B, and so forth.

Sentence cipher

Here is a different kind of alphabet cipher. You make up a sentence using all twenty-six letters of the alphabet without repeating any. The order in which the letters in your sentence come will make your secret alphabet.

To do this, write out your sentence and then write the alphabet over it. For example:

A   B   C   DEFGH   IJ   KL M   NOPQR   STU   V   WXYZ

V. F. X. BLITZ, JR., PH.D., KNOWS GUY Q. MACE

In this particular sentence cipher, the word SCHOOL would be written GXZNNH, because in the real alphabet the letter S falls over G, C over X, and so forth. When you want to decipher a message written with this sentence cipher, read from the letters of your secret sentence to the real alphabet above. Then you will see that G stands for S, X stands for C, and so on.

You will find that it is difficult to make sentences using all twenty-six letters of the alphabet without repeating any. But when you do make that kind of sentence, you can memorize it and carry your sentence cipher in your head without having to write it down.

13

The backward cipher

One more kind of alphabet cipher is the backward cipher.

Print the alphabet at the top of a sheet of paper, and beneath it print the alphabet backwards, beginning with Z, like this:

A	B	C	D	E	F	G	H	I	J	K	L	M	N	O	P	Q	R	S	T	U	V	W	X	Y	Z
Z	Y	X	W	V	U	T	S	R	Q	P	O	N	M	L	K	J	I	H	G	F	E	D	C	B	A

Draw lines between the letters, to separate A and Z from B and Y and so on. Z is now your cipher letter for A, Y is your cipher letter for B, and so on.

To encipher the word DANGER, for example, look below the D and you will see the letter W. W becomes the first letter of your enciphered message. Z is the letter below A, and so Z becomes the second letter of your enciphered message. The third letter is M, because it stands below N; T is below G, V below E, and I is below R. Your enciphered message looks like this: W Z M T V I.

To decipher this message, of course, you work the other way. Print both alphabets, and look for the letter *above* each letter in the enciphered message. To decipher the message D Z R G, for example, look for the letters above D and Z and R and G and you will see that the message reads WAIT.

14

A cipher found in the Bible

In the Bible there are several examples of the backward alphabet cipher. Ancient Hebrew prophets, thousands of years ago, used that cipher.

There is one example in the book of Jeremiah, chapter 25, verse 26. One word of that verse is in cipher—the word SHESHACH. It is a backward alphabet word for BABEL.

When you first look at those two words it may seem strange that a word of five letters can become a word of eight letters when it is put into the backward alphabet cipher. But the Hebrew alphabet is not like our alphabet. In Hebrew there is just one letter for our two letters SH, and one letter for our two letters CH.

The Hebrews called this cipher ATHBASH, because A was the first letter of their alphabet, TH was the last letter, B was the second letter, and SH was the second letter from the end. Calling their cipher ATHBASH was like calling our backward-alphabet cipher AZBY.

15

Number ciphers

You can write all sorts of secret messages by moving around in the alphabet, but you can also write messages without using any letters of the alphabet at all. You can use numbers instead.

Here is a very simple number cipher:

Print the alphabet across the top of a sheet of paper. Now, under each letter, write a number. Begin with the number 1 under the letter A, the number 2 under the letter B, and so on. Then draw lines to separate A and 1 from B and 2, like this:

A	B	C	D	E	F	G	H	I	J	K	L	M	N	O	P	Q	R	S	T	U	V	W	X	Y	Z
1	2	3	4	5	6	7	8	9	10	11	12	13	14	15	16	17	18	19	20	21	22	23	24	25	26

Now encipher a message by writing down the number below each letter, instead of the letter itself. To encipher the message SEE ME LATER, write down the number under S, the number under E, the number under E again, and then leave a space. Put little dashes between the numbers so that they will be easy to read. Then write down the number under M and the number under E. Leave another space, and then write down the numbers under the letters L, A, T, E, and R. Your enciphered message will look like this:

19-5-5   13-5   12-1-20-5-18

Practice this code by enciphering this message:

WHEN ARE YOU GOING HOME ?

Now decipher this message:

18-9-7-8-20   1-6-20-5-18   19-3-8-15-15-12

16

On answer page 57, you will find the first message correctly enciphered and the second one correctly deciphered.

There are many different number ciphers, just as there are many different alphabet ciphers. For example, you can number the alphabet backwards instead of forwards, beginning with 26 for A and ending with 1 for Z. Your cipher would look like this:

A	B	C	D	E	F	G	H	I	J	K	L	M	N	O	P	Q	R	S	T	U	V	W	X	Y	Z
26	25	24	23	22	21	20	19	18	17	16	15	14	13	12	11	10	9	8	7	6	5	4	3	2	1

Use the same method with this cipher that you did with the first number cipher. Simply encipher a message by writing the number beneath each letter in the message. For example, you would encipher the message WHAT TIME like this: 4-19-26-7   7-18-14-22.

Another kind of number cipher is numbering the alphabet by twos, like this:

A	B	C	D	E	F	G	H	I	J	K	L	M	N	O	P	Q	R	S	T	U	V	W	X	Y	Z
2	4	6	8	10	12	14	16	18	20	22	24	26	28	30	32	34	36	38	40	42	44	46	48	50	52

To encipher a message with this cipher, you again write down the number beneath each letter. You would encipher the message FOUR O'CLOCK, for example, like this: 12-30-42-36   30-6-24-30-6-22.

You can also invent your own secret number cipher. Just print the alphabet on a sheet of paper. Then, beneath each letter, write any number you want. A may be 324, B may be 5, C may be 57. Just be sure you don't use any number more than once.

Of course, if you invent a cipher like this, you will have to carry it around with you, because you probably won't be able to remember the number of each letter. And anybody who receives messages from you in this cipher will also have to have a copy of the cipher.

Be careful not to lose your cipher. If you do, it is a good idea to invent a new one immediately. Then if anyone finds your original cipher, he will not be able to read your messages.

The number-box cipher

A very good number cipher to use is the number-box cipher.

Draw lines to make five rows of boxes, with five boxes in each row, and write the letters of the alphabet in the boxes. Since you have only twenty-five boxes, and there are twenty-six letters in the alphabet, you will have to put two letters in one box. You can put I and J together, as J is not used very much.

Now number each crosswise row of boxes, from 1 to 5, and number the downward rows in the same way, so that your cipher looks like this:

	1	2	3	4	5
1	A	B	C	D	E
2	F	G	H	I J	K
3	L	M	N	O	P
4	Q	R	S	T	U
5	V	W	X	Y	Z

You are now ready to use the number-box cipher.

To encipher the letter A, first write down the number of the crosswise row in which that letter appears. This number is 1. Then write the number of the box in that row in which the letter appears. This number is also 1. So you encipher the letter A as 1-1, or 11, because it is in the number 1 crosswise row and in the number 1 box in that row.

Encipher the letter B as 12, because it is also in the number 1 crosswise row, but in the number 2 box in that row.

F is 21, L is 31, P is 35, R is 42, Z is 55, and so on.

Practice this cipher by enciphering this message:

ENEMY IS APPROACHING

Now decipher this message, written in the number-box cipher:

43-15-33-14   42-15-24-33-21-34-42-13-15-32-15-33-44-43

On answer page 58, you will find these messages correctly enciphered and deciphered.

19

Two famous early makers of codes

In the sixteenth century, codes were very popular among scholars. The scientists of that day often wrote to each other in code, so that ordinary people would not be able to read their messages and learn their secrets.

One of the famous code-makers of that time was Geronimo Cardano, who was born in Italy in the year 1501. He was an astrologer, a mathematician, and a fine doctor.

Cardano invented what he called the Trellis Cipher. When he wished to write secret messages to a friend, he took two sheets of stiff paper and cut holes in each one. The holes in one sheet of paper were exactly the same size and in exactly the same position as the holes in the other sheet. Each trellis, as he called it, looked

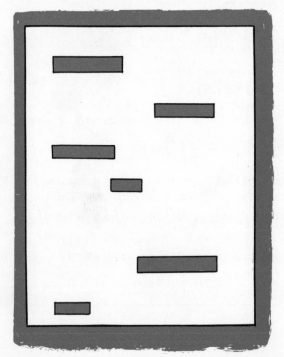

something like this drawing. Cardano then sent one trellis to his friend, and kept the other for himself.

When he wanted to write a message to his friend, he put his trellis over the clean sheet of paper, and wrote the secret message through the holes, putting one word in the top hole, one in the next lower one, and so on. Then he removed the trellis and filled up the rest of the paper

20

with other words. This had to be done very carefully, of course, so that the secret words would fit into the rest of the writing and seem to make sense. Cardano said, "You must try to compose an innocent-looking message to fill in the gaps."

When Cardano's friend received the message, he put his own trellis over the writing, and read just the few words that showed through the holes. Those words, he knew, were the secret message his friend was sending him.

Here is an example of a message written with Cardano's Trellis Cipher. The words enclosed in boxes are the ones written through the holes of the trellis:

My dear Friend,:
Have you heard the news? The King of Naples will soon make a visit to Rome. As for me, I prefer as usual to remain at home, especially now when it will soon be fine weather here. But I suppose it is necessary for the King to go, as Rome will not come to him. The seeds in my garden are now all secretly swelling in the earth, and the swallows have arrived, so I know spring is close by. I hope your garden too does well, and that you enjoy good health by day and sound sleep by night.
                                        G. Cardano

Another famous code-maker of the sixteenth century was Giambattista della Porta, an Italian scientist born in 1538. He wrote a book about secret codes, and has been called by some people the Father of Modern Cryptography. **Cryptography,** a word made up out of the Greek words *kryptos*, meaning "secret," and *graphos,* meaning "writing," is the scientific name for the study of codes and ciphers. A person who uses codes or ciphers is called a **cryptographer.**

One of the curious codes in Porta's book is called a box-and-dot code (even though it is really a cipher).

A box-and-dot code

Here is a code that doesn't use letters or numbers. Instead it uses simple little designs that look very mysterious. In this box-and-dot code, as it is called, the message WAIT FOR ME looks like this:

But even though this code looks strange, it is easy to learn. Draw three sets of criss-crossed lines, as if you were going to play three games of tick-tack-toe. In the second set put a dot in each square, or box. In the third set put two dots in each box. Then write the letters of the alphabet in the boxes, starting with A in the top left-hand corner of the first set and filling the boxes one by one. Your code will look like this:

Now look closely at the box where you have written the A. If that box were broken off from the first set of lines, it would look like this: ⌐A⌐. Remove the A and you have ⌐⌐ which is your code for the letter A. The code for your letter B is the shape of the box the B is in. It looks like this: ⌐⌐ . The code for the letter C is the shape of the box C is in, and looks like this: ⌐ .

Code signs for the rest of the letters of the alphabet are made in the same way, except that the letters from J through R have a dot inside the box, and the letters from S through Z have two dots. Here is the box-and-dot code for the whole alphabet:

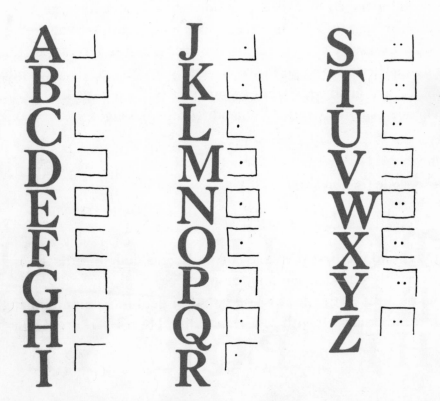

You will notice that the bottom right-hand box in the third set of criss-crossed lines is empty, because your three sets of lines give you 27 squares and there are only 26 letters in the alphabet. This empty square can be very useful. You might let it stand for the word *and,* or for some other word that you use often in secret messages. Then instead of spelling that word out when you come to it, you can use the code sign instead.

If you want to send the message CODE CLUB MEETING TODAY in this code, it will look like this:

⌞⊡⊐☐ ⌞⌞⊡⊡⊔ ⊐☐☐⊔⌈⊡⊓ ⊔⊡⊐⌐⊓

This box-and-dot code, like the number-box code (or cipher), is especially handy because you don't have to memorize it or carry it around with you. Whenever you want to encode or decode a message, you can draw the tick-tack-toe boxes, put the dots and letters in, and go to work. And you can destroy the code when you are finished, so that no one else will ever see it.

Practice using this code by encoding this message:

COME TO MY HOUSE

Now decode this message:

⊐⊡ ⊔⊡⊔ ⊓⊡ ⌈⊡⊐☐

You will find the first message correctly encoded, and the second one correctly decoded, on answer page 58.

The box-and-dot code was used a great deal in England during the fifteenth and sixteenth centuries, when Henry VII and Henry

VIII were on the throne. People who were plotting against the king, or on the king's side against England's enemy, France, often used this code for sending secret messages. Cardinal Thomas Wolsey, an adviser to King Henry VIII, used a form of this code for the messages which he sent.

The semaphore code

If you belong to the Scouts you may already know how to spell out words by holding your arms in certain positions. Each position is the code for a certain letter. Holding both arms straight out from the shoulder, for example, is the code position for the letter R. Dropping the right arm straight down, and leaving the left one sticking straight out, is the code position for the letter F. This method of sending messages is called semaphore, and if you don't know it you can learn it by looking at the next two pages.

When you know the semaphore code you can easily send messages across a big field, or across several back yards. If you want to send messages for an even greater distance, you can hold a brightly colored flag in each hand. The flags will make it possible for someone to "read" your messages even if you are quite a long way away. If you want to send a message in the dark, you can hold a lighted flashlight in each hand.

25

You can use the semaphore code for sending written messages, too. Use a small straight line to represent each arm, and a tiny circle to represent the shoulders, where the two arms join. A circle with a line going straight out on each side of it, for example, is the code for the letter R.

Turn back to the pages showing the semaphore code, and you will see underneath each letter the code for writing that letter.

The message HELP FIRE can be written in the semaphore code like this:

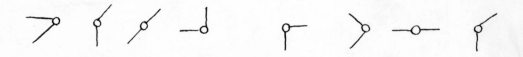

Practice this code by signaling these messages with your arms, and by writing them down:

CAMP HERE

ALL PATROLS COME IN

Now decode these messages:

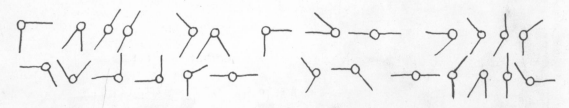

On answer page 58, you will find the messages correctly encoded and decoded.

28

The Morse code

The Morse code is an international code—one known all over the world. It was invented by Samuel F. B. Morse, and it is still used by telegraph and radio operators. They use it by clicking out dots and dashes on a little key. A click followed by a short space, or rest, is the signal for a dot. A click followed by a longer space, or rest, is the signal for a dash.

The Morse code signal for the letter A is dot-dash. The signal for the letter B is dash-dot-dot-dot.

Here are the Morse code signals for the whole alphabet:

A • —	J • — — —	S • • •
B — • • •	K — • —	T —
C — • — •	L • — • •	U • • —
D — • •	M — —	V • • • —
E •	N — •	W • — —
F • • — •	O — — —	X — • • —
G — — •	P • — — •	Y — • — —
H • • • •	Q — — • —	Z — — • •
I • •	R • — •	

If you learn the Morse code you will find it very useful. You can use it for written messages, like this one:

• — —/• • • •/• /— •/— •//• • /• • •//• — —•/• /• — • •/• — /— •/• //— • •/• • —/• //

Can you decode that message? Then encode this message:

PLANE   ARRIVING   AT   SIX

You will find these messages correctly decoded and encoded on answer page 59.

But you can use the Morse code in other ways too. You can click out messages to your friends. Outdoors use a stick against a tin can. Indoors click with your fingernail or with a pencil on a table or the arm of a chair. Make a click with a short rest after it for a dot, and a click with a longer rest after it for a dash. Use a longer pause to show that you have come to the end of a word. Clicking out the Morse code with your fingernail is a good way to have a secret conversation with someone in a room. Probably the other people in the room won't even realize that you are sending a secret message.

Native African tribes signal to each other by beating out messages on drums, in a code something like the Morse code. This drum code system has been called the "bush telegraph."

The ogams of the Celts

Before the Romans conquered part of Britain, that country had been overrun by a sturdy people called Celts, who had first lived along the northern slopes of the Alps and had once been so powerful that in the year 390 B.C. they invaded the city of Rome.

It was probably in Rome that the Celts learned the Latin, or Roman, alphabet, which is the foundation of our own alphabet today. And when they invented their own kind of secret writing they invented a cipher for the letters of that alphabet. Their curious cipher letters are called **ogams**, and can be seen today on stone monuments in the British Isles.

When a man wanted to write a message in ogams, he first drew —or chiseled in stone—a long straight line. Then he wrote the letters of the message by drawing shorter lines up to, or across that one long line. Here are the ogams of the Celts:

You could invent a very interesting cipher by using the signs of the Celts, but adding enough more to make them fit our own alphabet. If you also rearranged your letters to run from A to Z in regular order, your cipher would look like this:

A B C D E F G H I J K L M N O P Q R S T U V W X Y Z

You might call this cipher the modern ogam cipher.

Here is a message written in this modern ogam cipher:

Can you decipher the message? You will find the correct answer on answer page 59.

Breaking the cipher of the Spanish king

When Henry IV was King of France, in the sixteenth century, his most powerful enemy was the King of Spain. When Henry's secret police captured Spanish messengers they often found the Spaniards carrying bits of paper covered with rows of tiny mysterious signs. Finally, after seeing several of these strange bits of paper, Henry decided that the tiny signs were a kind of cipher—that each sign stood for a certain letter of the alphabet. He also decided that any message written in cipher must be very important, and that if he knew what the messages said he would know a great deal about his enemy's plans.

So the French King sent for a professor of mathematics. The professor's name was François Viète, and he is famous today as the Father of Algebra. King Henry told him to try to read the message.

Viète succeeded. He broke the Spanish cipher, by figuring out which letter of the alphabet each of the tiny signs represented.

For the next two years the French seized every Spanish message they could find, gave it to Viète to read, and then sent the message on its way. Finally the King of Spain realized that the King of France knew what was written in his secret messages. He realized that his secret cipher was no longer secret. But he couldn't understand what had happened. He was sure no human being could ever figure out what those mysterious signs stood for, and so he decided that the French King must have had supernatural help—that the Devil himself had aided him.

The truth was, of course, that King Henry of France had been aided only by the mathematics expert. And this is important to remember, because even today the breaking of ciphers is done with the help of mathematics. You have to do a great deal of counting if you want to break a cipher. But we have learned that, as experts say, "Any cipher man can make, a man can break."

33

How to break a cipher

It is not easy to break a cipher. Usually it is a job for an expert, for someone who has studied ciphers a long time. But there are certain clues that will help you to break many ciphers. The clues can be found in the way our words are spelled, and in the number of times certain letters are usually used.

The first and most important clue is the frequency with which letters appear. The letter E, for example, is the most common letter in the English language. In almost every ordinary message, or in almost every page of printed or written words, the letter E appears oftener than any other letter.

Here are the ten most frequently used letters in the alphabet in the order of their frequency:

E   T   A   O   N   R   I   S   H   D

Another important clue is found in "double" letters. These are letters that are used in pairs, as in the words roLL, mEEt, tOOl, cLASS, and so forth. The letters most often doubled are:

LL   EE   SS   OO   TT

GO   SAFE CAMP   GENTLEMEN   DOCTOR

A third important clue is found in those combinations of two different letters which often appear together. The combination TH, for example, appears in each of these words: THat, THis, THing, paTH. Two-letter combinations which most often appear are, in their order of frequency:

TH   HE   AN   RE   ER   IN

A fourth clue is found in the combinations of three different letters which often appear together. The combination THE, for example, is a word by itself, but it also appears in many other words, such as oTHEr, faTHEr, togeTHEr. The combination ING appears in many words too, such as sING, goING, walkING, and so forth. Three-letter combinations which most often appear are, in order of frequency:

THE   ING   AND   ION   ENT

One more important clue is the fact that if you see one letter standing alone, it is almost sure to be either A or I. That is why many code experts first encipher a message and then break it up into groups of five letters each, instead of writing it in separate words. You will see why this makes it more difficult to decipher a message if you break up the sentence I WILL NOT COME TO YOUR HOUSE into groups of five letters each, running words together or breaking them in the middle if necessary. Then that sentence looks like this: IWILL NOTCO METOY OURHO USEAX.

KIND WOMAN

BAD DOG

VERY GOOD   OFFICER

ALL RIGH

The two letters added at the end, to make the last "word" five letters long, are called **nulls** and are a favorite trick of cryptographers. That sentence, written in five-letter groups, almost looks like a secret code message itself.

Of course in a very short message, or in a message full of technical words or other kinds of special words, the four important clues listed on the preceding two pages may not help to break a cipher. Even though E is the most common letter in our language, it is possible to write a sentence with no E's in it at all, such as THIS SHIP SAILS SWIFTLY.

If somebody enciphered that sentence and sent it to you, you would have trouble breaking the cipher because your most important clue would give you no help at all.

But let's see how we might use these clues if you received a message in cipher, and didn't know which cipher had been used. Let's say the message reads:

UIF   FOFNZ   BSF   PO   XBZ   DPNF   BU   PODF   BMM
TFU   GPS   BUUBDL   UPOJHIU

We notice that the message is in ordinary words, not broken up into five-letter groups. This will make it easier, especially as the message contains two two-letter words. Two-letter words are sometimes easy to guess. So let's get right to work.

First we make a list of the letters of the alphabet, and write

36

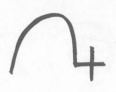

GUARDED HOUSE   STOP   DANGER   MAN WITH GUN

alongside each letter the number of times that letter appears in the message. We find that there are no A's in the message at all, that there are 6 B's, and so on. Our list looks like this:

A—	H—1	O—4	V—
B—6	I—2	P—5	W—
C—	J—1	Q—	X—1
D—3	K—	R—	Y—
E—	L—1	S—2	Z—2
F—7	M—2	T—1	
G—1	N—2	U—7	

Our list shows that the letter F and U appear most often in the message. Each appears 7 times. So probably either F or U stands for that usually most-common letter E. Now we are ready to begin the trial-and-error guessing method by which all ciphers are solved, even by the best experts.

First we copy the enciphered message on a large sheet of paper, leaving plenty of room between the lines. Then we put an E below every F in the enciphered message. If that proves wrong we will try putting an E below every U in the message instead.

UIF   FOFNZ   BSF   PO   XBZ   DPNF   BU   PODF   BMM
   E   E E   E   E   E

TFU   GPS   BUUBDL   UPOJHIU

Now we look at the list of most-frequent letters on page 34 and

BE QUIET   DON'T GIVE UP   JUDGE   TELL PITIFUL STORY

see that T is the next most common letter after E. So we decide that if F stands for E, maybe the U's in the secret message stand for T's. So we put a T below every U in the message.

UIF	FOFNZ	BSF	PO	XBZ	DPNF	BU	PODF	BMM
T E	E E	E			E	T	E	

TFU	GPS	BUUBDL	UPOJHIU
ET		TT	T T

So far it looks quite hopeful. In fact we now have two more interesting clues. One is in the first word, which reads T_E. It can't be TAE or TBE or TCE, because there are no such words. But if we go on through the alphabet, trying each letter in turn in that empty space, we come to the word THE. Those three letters might also turn out to be TEE, TIE or TOE, but THE is a more common word than any of those, so let's try it first. If we use H for the middle letter in that word, which means that we are writing H for the I in the enciphered message, then we will decipher every other I in the message as H too. We find just one more, in the last word of the message.

Our second new clue is in the little two-letter word written BU in the cipher. As we have decided to decipher the U as a T, it now reads _T. The word must be either AT or IT, because there are no ordinary two-letter words which end in T except those two. Let's experiment first with AT, and fill in A's for every other B in the

38

DRAG F   CROSS O   ROCKING H   HAT A   SITTING HEART-LAZY B

message. **Now we have:**

UIF	FOFNZ	BSF	PO	XBZ	DPNF	BU	PODF	BMM
THE	E E	A E		A		E	AT	E	A

TFU	GPS	BUUBDL	UPOJHIU
ET		ATTA	T	HT

Now we have another clue, in the three-letter word BSF partly deciphered into A_E. If we try filling in the empty space with various letters, we find that the word ARE is more common than any of the other words we can make, so let's write an R in place of the S, as an experiment. And let's write R's for every other S in the message. Now we have:

UIF	FOFNZ	BSF	PO	XBZ	DPNF	BU	PODF	BMM
THE	E E	ARE		A		E	AT	E	A

TFU	GPS	BUUBDL	UPOJHIU
ET	R	ATTA	T	HT

There is another clue waiting for us now in the word BUUBDL. We have deciphered the B's into A's, and the U's into T's, so we have ATTA_ _. The word might be ATTACK, so let's put C's for the other D's in the message, and K for the L, too:

UIF	FOFNZ	BSF	PO	XBZ	DPNF	BU	PODF	BMM
THE	E E	ARE		A	C	E	AT	CE	A

TFU	GPS	BUUBDL	UPOJHIU
ET	R	ATTACK	T	HT

CATTLEBRANDS

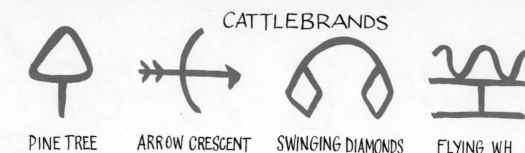

PINE TREE   ARROW CRESCENT   SWINGING DIAMONDS   FLYING WH

Now go back to the list of most-frequent letters. The letters E, T and A, usually the most frequent, are already decoded. The list tells us that the next-most-frequent letter is likely to be O, and the one after that is N. If we look at the count we made of the most frequent letters in our cipher message, we find that the fourth most frequent one is P and the fifth is O. Let's see what happens if we decipher every P as an O and every O as an N. Now we have:

UIF	FOFNZ	BSF	PO	XBZ	DPNF	BU	PODF	BMM
THE	ENE	ARE	ON	A	CO E	AT	ONCE	A

TFU	GPS	BUUBDL	UPOJHIU
ET	OR	ATTACK	TON HT

Our little two-letter word PO is ON, and the four-letter word PODF is ONCE. We can be pretty sure we are right about P and O.

Now the sixth, seventh and eighth words of the message read CO_E AT ONCE. Surely that is COME AT ONCE. And if we decoded that one N into an M, we can do the same for the N in the second word, which gives us ENEM_.That word must be ENEMY. Now we can put a Y in the place of the other Z, in that three-letter ciphered word XBZ, which will give us _AY. Let's take a careful look at the first eight words of the message. They read THE ENEMY ARE ON _AY COME AT ONCE. _AY must be WAY.

Now let's look at the two words before the last word of the secret message. They read _OR ATTACK. By trying different letters of

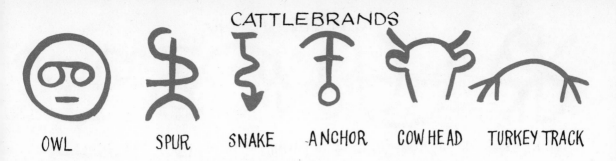

OWL   SPUR   SNAKE   -ANCHOR   COW HEAD   TURKEY TRACK

the alphabet in the blank space we find that _OR could be FOR or NOR, but FOR ATTACK sounds more likely, so let's make the enciphered G an F.

How about that curious little three-letter word BMM? So far we know only that the first letter is A. Let's look at the list of most-frequent double letters and see if we can decide what the MM stands for. The only word that really makes sense is ALL. So let's write that in. Now we have:

UIF	FOFNZ	BSF	PO	XBZ	DPNF	BU	PODF	BMM
THE	ENEMY	ARE	ON	WAY	COME	AT	ONCE	ALL

TFU	GPS	BUUBDL	UPOJHIU
ET	FOR	ATTACK	TON HT

The entire message is deciphered now except for the two words that read _ET and TON_ _HT. We look at our list of most-frequent letters again, and in the list we find that I and S are the two next most-frequent letters after the ones we have already used—E, T, A, O, N and R. So let's see if an I or an S fits into any of those blanks.

Soon we discover that our whole message reads:

THE	ENEMY	ARE	ON	WAY	COME	AT	ONCE	ALL
SET	FOR	ATTACK	TONIGHT					

We have broken the cipher!

Of course we were lucky in deciphering this message because we made the right choice in the beginning. We had two most-

41

DOUBLE R   ED CONNECTED   DHP CONNECTED   03   FLYING JY

frequent letters in our secret message, the letters F and U, and we had no way of knowing which of those letters stood for E. If we had tried E's in place of all the U's in the beginning, instead of trying E's in place of all the F's, we might have worked for quite a while before we discovered that we were off on the wrong track. Getting off on the wrong track is always possible in deciphering and it wastes a lot of time. That's why people who decipher secret messages have to have a great deal of patience and be willing to start over many times if their first efforts don't bring success.

By now, of course, you have figured out which alphabet cipher was used for this message. It was the first cipher explained in this book: B was used for A, C for B and so on, with the next letter in the alphabet always used for each letter in the original message.

An expert would have deciphered our secret message much faster than we did. As soon as he discovered that F was apparently being used for E, and U for T, he would have guessed which cipher was being used and would probably have deciphered the whole message in just a few minutes.

It takes a lot of practice and training to become an expert. In the United States Army, for example, men go to a special school and study for several months to become cryptographers.

But anybody can learn to encipher messages, and anybody who has patience can enjoy the game of trying to decipher them.

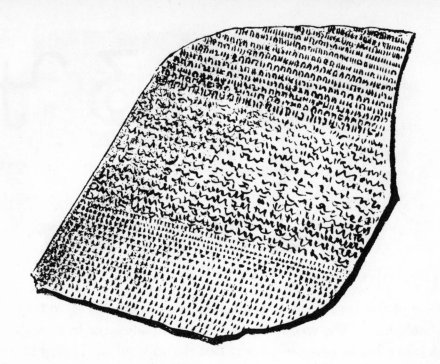

The Rosetta Stone

One of the most famous examples of deciphering is that of the Rosetta Stone. The Rosetta Stone is a piece of black basalt which was found in Egypt in 1799. On it is writing in three different scripts: Greek, Egyptian hieroglyphics, and another form of ancient Egyptian writing. Up until that time no one had been able to read Egyptian hieroglyphics, but people knew how to read Greek. Scholars figured out that the three different writings said the same thing, so working from the Greek, which they knew, they eventually "decoded" the Egyptian hieroglyphics. Once these hieroglyphics were worked out, other hieroglyphic inscriptions could be read, too.

The Rosetta Stone was carved in 196 B.C., and is now in the British Museum in London.

Invisible inks

One of the best ways to send a secret message is to write it in invisible ink. If the wrong person sees your message he will think it is just a blank piece of paper. But if you send the message to a friend who also knows the secret of invisible ink, the friend will know how to make the message become visible. He will just heat the paper and suddenly the writing will appear as if by magic.

George Washington's spies sometimes used invisible ink for their secret messages, instead of writing those messages in code.

Invisible ink is easy to use, and it is easy to prepare because it can be made from things you probably have in your house all the time. Here are several different kinds of invisible ink:

LEMON JUICE INK—Squeeze the juice of half a lemon into a small dish or glass. The lemon juice makes an excellent invisible ink. **ORANGE JUICE INK** and **GRAPEFRUIT JUICE INK** can be made in the same way.

44

SUGAR WATER INK—Put half a tea-spoonful of sugar into half a glass of water and stir until the sugar is completely dissolved.

HONEY WATER INK—Put half a tea-spoonful of honey into half a glass of water and stir until the honey is dissolved and the water is clear.

ONION JUICE INK—Peel a small onion, grate it into a pulp, and let the pulp stand in a small dish or glass. At the end of several minutes you will see that part of the pulp has become liquid. This liquid is an excellent invisible ink.

SODA POP INK—Put two teaspoonfuls of soda pop into a small dish or glass, add one teaspoonful of water, and stir. You can try using soda pop alone as an ink, but you will probably find that writing done with pure soda pop is not completely invisible.

The best way to write with invisible ink is to use an ordinary pen point. Be sure it is clean before you dip it into your invisible ink. A toothpick makes a good invisible-ink pen too, but you will have to dip it into the ink after each word you write, because the toothpick will not hold very much ink.

WARNING !
DO NOT USE A FOUNTAIN PEN OR A BALL-POINT PEN

You can write invisible-ink messages on any kind of white paper that is good for regular ink.

Of course you cannot see the words you write after you have written them, except during the few seconds that the paper looks wet where the ink is. So you will have to be careful to make sure you do not write one word on top of another. When you stop writing for a moment, to dip your pen into the ink, put a finger at the end of the last word you wrote, so you will know where to begin the next word. If you use paper with lines printed on it, the lines will help you keep your invisible writing straight.

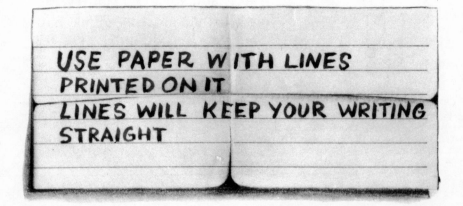

To make invisible writing become visible, heat the paper. There are several ways to do this:

Hold the paper against the hottest part—that is, against the top—of a lighted 60-watt bulb. In less than half a minute your writing will begin to appear. The writing will be brown. Move the paper around until every part of it has become warm and all the writing has become visible. Do not hold the paper against the bulb too long, or the paper will turn brown too.

Or hold the paper near a fairly hot electric iron.

Or hold the paper, part of it at a time, over the slots of an electric pop-up toaster.

A very good way to send messages in invisible ink is to write the invisible messages between the lines of an ordinary note or letter, written with regular ink or pencil. Write the ordinary mes-

47

sage first, like this, leaving plenty of space between the lines:

Dear John: I have to mow the lawn this afternoon,

so I will not be able to go fishing with you.

Arthur

Now, between the lines, write the secret message. If anybody except John sees the message, he will think you are not able to go fishing. But John knows that your note may hide a secret message, written in invisible ink, so he heats the paper against a lighted bulb, or an electric iron, or over a toaster, and this is what he sees:

Dear John: I have to mow the lawn this afternoon
I mowed the lawn yesterday, so I will meet
so I will not be able to go fishing with you
you at the fishing hole at half past three
Arthur

You can also write your invisible-ink messages in code, so that even if somebody knows the trick of invisible ink and is able to read your message, he won't know what it means.

Codes used in the world's work

Storekeepers often use codes to write secret numbers on things they sell. Store codes are very simple. A storekeeper chooses a word that has ten different letters in it, and lets each letter of that word stand for a number, like this:

I M P O R T A N C E
1 2 3 4 5 6 7 8 9 0

If the storekeeper writes IRE on a hammer, for example, that tells him that he paid $1.50 for it, and from that he knows how much to charge his customers. Other words storekeepers use for their codes, because they are also made up of ten different letters, are PRUDENTIAL, REPUBLICAN and DUMBWAITER. This storekeeper code is good to use for encoding numbers of any kind.

Businessmen very often used to use codes in their cable messages to other countries, because each word in a cable message cost a great deal. By using codes in which one word or one group of four or five letters stood for several words, or even for a whole sentence, they could save a great deal of money. Usually they invented code words instead of using real words.

The code word ABCAB, for example, might stand for the two words "Order received." The code word ABDOD might stand for "Shipment ready for immediate delivery." By sending a cable which read ABCAB ABDOD, a businessman would have to pay for only two words, but his customer would know the cable really said "Order received. Shipment ready for immediate delivery."

However, when the cost of each word in a cable message fell very sharply some years ago, and when international telephone and radio and teletype service became common, many businessmen stopped using codes altogether.

A secret language

Can you understand this secret message:

OMECAY OVERWAY OTWAY YMAY OUSEHAY?

If you can read that sentence you can speak one of the most famous secret languages in the world: **Pig Latin.** Pig Latin sounds very strange when you speak it, and looks strange when you write it down, but it is not hard to learn.

Look at the secret message on this page again and you will notice one very important thing about it: every word ends with the same two letters, AY. When you speak Pig Latin you put those two letters at the end of every word you say.

But now look at the first word in that message, the word OMECAY. Take off the AY and you have OMEC. Then take the last letter of the word, the C, and move it to the front of the word, and you have the simple word COME.

Now you can see how easy it is to put the word COME into Pig Latin. You just take the first letter off and put it at the end of the word, and then add the two letters AY.

The third word in the secret message, OTAY, was put into Pig Latin the same way. The word was TO. The T was put at the end of the word, instead of at the beginning, and the letters AY were added.

Now you can figure out the last word in the message for yourself. Take off the AY from OUSEHAY and you have OUSEH. Take the H off the end of the word and put it at the beginning and you have HOUSE.

And now you know one of the two simple rules of Pig Latin: When a word begins with a consonant (a consonant is any letter except a, e, i, o, u), take off the first letter, put it at the end of the word, and then add AY.

The only time you may have trouble with this rule is when a word begins with QU or with groups of two or more consonants together, like CH, BR, PL, SC, SCH, or SCR. When you want to use words like that, move the entire first group of letters to the end of the word, and then add the letters AY, like this:

children becomes ildrenchay
question becomes estionquay
cry becomes ycray
school becomes oolschay
true becomes uetray

The second rule for speaking Pig Latin is easier than the first: when a word begins with a vowel—(the vowels are a, e, i, o, u) just add the three letters WAY to the end of the word. The word AT, for example, becomes ATWAY. The word ELEVATOR becomes ELEVATORWAY. I becomes IWAY, and IS becomes ISWAY.

Now you can see that the second word in the secret message on page 51, the word OVERWAY, is just the word OVER with the three letters WAY added on the end.

To practice this secret language put these sentences into Pig Latin:

WHERE WILL YOU BE AFTER SCHOOL ?

WHAT TIME IS IT ?

CAN YOU GO TO THE MOVIES ?

Look on answer page 59 to see if you have put the sentences into Pig Latin correctly.

It is more fun to speak Pig Latin than to write it, and with a little practice you will be able to speak it very quickly. And here is a good thing to remember: any foreign language can be a secret language between two people who know it. If somebody in your family knows Spanish or Italian or French, ask them to teach you a few words of it, and then teach those words to a friend. You two will be able to say things to each other that most people can't understand.

During World War II the Army used Navaho Indians for sending secret messages back and forth from one part of a battlefield to another. One Indian just shouted the message in the Navaho language to another Indian, and the enemy never knew what they were saying.

53

Two famous stories about codes and ciphers

   Edgar Allan Poe is one of the many famous writers who were
much interested in codes and ciphers, and used them in their
stories. One of Poe's best-known is *The Gold Bug,* in which a
man finds a message written in cipher on a torn piece of parch-
ment buried in the sand along the shore. He decodes the message
and it tells him where to find a great chest full of pirate gold and
jewels.

Sir Arthur Conan Doyle, who wrote many stories about his famous detective character, Sherlock Holmes, also used a cipher in one of his best-known stories. The story is called *The Adventure of the Dancing Men*. In that story, Holmes decodes messages made up of tiny figures which look like dancing men. Holmes decides that each different kind of figure represents a different letter, and that the rows of dancing men are really rows of letters, or words. Here is one word written in the cipher of the dancing men:

Holmes decoded this word as NEVER.

A final message

If you are interested in the subject, you may also want to read other books about codes and ciphers and invisible writing. A very good book to read is *Codes and Secret Writing,* by Herbert S. Zim.

And now perhaps you would like to try deciphering a message from the very beginning. You can check your answer with the solution on answer page 59.

PQY VJCV AQW JCXG TGCF VJKU DQQM, AQW

UJQWNF DG CDNG VQ TGCF VJKU OGUUCIG:

IQQF NWEM CPF JCRRA EQFKPI

ANSWER PAGE

From page 6:

C L U B   M E E T I N G   T O D A Y
D M V C   N F F U J O H   U P E B Z

C A L L   F O R   M E   O N   S A T U R D A Y
D B M M   G P S   N F   P O   T B U V S E B Z

X I F S F   J T   U I F   Q J D O J D
W H E R E   I S   T H E   P I C N I C

From page 11:

I S   Y O U R   H O M E W O R K   D O N E
K U   A Q W T   J Q O G Y Q T M   F Q P G

K   H K P K U J G F   V J G   D Q Q M
I   F I N I S H E D   T H E   B O O K

From page 16:

W H E N   A R E   Y O U   G O I N G   H O M E
23- 8- 5- 14   1- 18- 5   25-15-21   7- 15- 9- 14- 7   8- 15- 13- 5

18- 9- 7- 8- 20   1- 6- 20- 5- 18   19- 3- 8- 15- 15- 12
R I G H T   A F T E R   S C H O O L

From page 19:

E N E M Y   I S   A P P R O A C H I N G
15- 33- 15- 32- 54   24-43   11- 35- 35- 42- 34- 11- 13- 23- 24- 33- 22

43- 15- 33- 14   42- 15- 24- 33- 21- 34- 42- 13- 15- 32- 15- 33- 44- 43

S E N D   R E I N F O R C E M E N T S

From page 24:

C O M E   T O   M Y   H O U S E

M U S T   G O   H O M E

From page 28:

C A M P   H E R E

A L L   P A T R O L S   C O M E   I N

F A L L   I N   F O R   H I K E

S U P P E R   I S   R E A D Y

From page 29:

•— —/•••/•/—•//••/•••//•—— •/•—••/•—/—•/•/—•/•//—••/••—/•//

W H E N	I S	P L A N E	D U E	

P L A N E	A R R I V I N G	A T	S I X

•— —•/•—••/•—/—•/•//•—/•—•/•—•/••/••—/•—•/—/•/—•/——•//•—/—/// •••/••/—••—//

From page 32:

T H E   R O M A N S   A R E   C O M I N G

From page 53:

WHERE	WILL	YOU	BE	AFTER	SCHOOL
EREWHAY	ILLWAY	OUYAY	EBAY	AFTERWAY	OOLSCHAY

WHAT	TIME	IS	IT
ATWHAY	IMETAY	ISWAY	ITWAY

CAN	YOU	GO	TO	THE	MOVIES
ANCAY	OUYAY	OGAY	OTAY	ETHAY	OVIESMAY

From page 56:

PQY	VJCV	AQW	JCXG	TGCF	VJKU	DQQM	AQW
NOW	THAT	YOU	HAVE	READ	THIS	BOOK,	YOU

UJQWNF	DG	CDNG	VQ	TGCF	VJKU	OGUUCIG:
SHOULD	BE	ABLE	TO	READ	THIS	MESSAGE:

IQQF	NWEM	CPF	JCRRA	EQFKPI
GOOD	LUCK	AND	HAPPY	CODING

Index

About the Authors:

Not one clicking typewriter but *two*—that's the way it is in the Epstein home. **SAM** and **BERYL EPSTEIN** worked as a writing team even before their marriage in 1938. Since then, individually or in collaboration, they have written a good-sized shelf of books as full-time authors.

The Epsteins have a home in New York City, but they prefer their cottage at Mattituck, L. I., where fishing, digging clams and gardening are a pleasant change from the literary life.

About the Artist:

LÁSZLO ROTH, whose entertaining illustrations decorate these pages, was born in Hungary and has lived in Latin America as well as in this country. He has illustrated many other books. His work appears regularly in *The New Yorker* and other magazines.

D B M M   G P S   N F

23 - 8 - 5 - 14   1 - 18 - 5

N F F U   N F   B G U F S   T D I P P M

A T W H A Y   I M E T A Y

15 - 33 - 15 - 32 - 54   24 - 43

PO TBUVSEBZ

25-15-21 7-15-9-14-7

XIFSF JT UIF QJDOJD

IS WAY ITWAY

11- 35- 35- 42- 34- 11- 13- 23- 24- 33- 22